This book belongs to

_____

Learning To Slow Down and Pay Attention

Revised Edition

Written by Kathleen G. Nadeau, Ph.D. and
Ellen B. Dixon, Ph.D.
Illustrated by John R. Rose

Published by

Chesapeake Psychological Publications
A Division of Chesapeake Psychological Services, P.C.

Learning to Slow Down and Pay Attention.

Revised Edition 1993

Chesapeake Psychological Publications' titles may be ordered
through local bookstores or direct from the publisher. For direct
orders, add $1.25 for the first copy, 50¢ for each additional copy
to 4, and for 5 copies or more add $3.00 shipping and handling.
Virginia residents please add appropriate sales tax. Quantity
discounts are available for groups and organizations. For more
information, write to:

Special Sales Department
Chesapeake Psychological Publications
5041 A & B Backlick Road
Annandale, VA 22003
(703) 642-6697

ISBN 1-883030-02-1

Acknowledgements

We would like to express our appreciation to the many parents and children who have shared their experiences with us and helped us develop the ideas for this book. Our grateful thanks go also to Patricia Quinn, M.D. of Chevy Chase, Maryland who shared her expertise, and who generously took time from her busy schedule to offer suggestions, encouragement, and editorial input. We are also indebted to Melvin D. Levine, M.D., of the Clinical Center for the Study of Development and Learning at the University of North Carolina at Chapel Hill, who gave the valuable suggestion to steer away from using the more narrow ADD or ADHD label and to focus instead on the more general issues of problems of attention and concentration. Finally, we would like to extend our thanks to Beverly Horn and Terri Kunze who have patiently and painstakingly translated our various scribbles through countless drafts to this final version.

To Our Colleagues & Adult Helpers:

We've divided this book into four sections: the introduction and checklist, the description of interventions, practical ideas for help at home, and a new fourth section of worksheets and activity pages. We suggest that you read the book along with your child and that you go through only one section at a sitting, pausing to discuss various points and ideas wherever this seems useful. The third section, which focuses on things your child can learn to do to help himself, should be used repeatedly as a resource as your child gradually builds skills in these areas. And finally, in the back of this edition, we have added some special notes to children and parents, along with worksheets and new activity pages. At the end of each section is an activity, which we hope will end the session on a relaxed and upbeat note for your child.

You may notice as you read this book with your child that we have avoided the ADD or ADHD label. We have done this for several reasons. As more and more research is done with both children and adults, we realize that we are dealing with a very complex set of neurodevelopmental issues which are inadequately described by the ADHD label. There is a great deal of variety among children who are currently labeled ADHD. Other children who manifest significant attentional difficulties do not meet the strict criteria for an ADHD diagnosis, and yet these children are in great need of assistance and intervention. By avoiding the label, we can address the needs of all children with problems of attention, impulsivity, and concentration.

Just as importantly, we don't want to suggest to your child that he has a disease called "ADHD." Rather than learning to identify himself by a label, what your child needs is to gain an understanding of his particular issues concerning attention, impulsivity, and hyperactivity, and what can be done to assist him with those issues.

We hope this new addition will be an enjoyable way for your child to learn about him or herself and to begin the lifelong process of self-understanding and self-help.

Kathleen G. Nadeau, Ph.D., and
Ellen B. Dixon, Ph.D.

To Our Young Readers:

Our names are Kathleen Nadeau and Ellen Dixon. We are psychologists who work with boys and girls. Some of these kids have trouble paying attention in school or getting their homework finished at home. Some of the kids we see are very active and have trouble sitting still in school all day. Other kids may get into trouble because they do things before they stop and think. If you have any of these difficulties, we hope this book can help you understand more about yourself and about some of the things that can help you.

We'd like you to read this book with your mom or dad so that you can talk with them about what you're reading. There are lots of books for teachers and parents. We thought that kids deserved one, too. So this is just for you.

PART ONE

THE BEGINNING
My Own Check List

Lots of kids, and grown-ups too, have trouble concentrating, listening, and remembering. Some people have so much extra energy that it's almost like their "motor" runs too fast and can't turn off. If you are like this, probably someone else in your family is like this too, because these traits "run" in families.

Your brain may work in a slightly different way that makes it harder for you to pay attention, to listen, and to remember.

We've talked to lots of kids with these difficulties. All of these kids are a little different from each other. The next part of our book tells you some of the things they have said about themselves. We would like you to read each comment with your mom or dad. Make a check mark in the box next to each comment that is just like you.

Like this:

After the checklists, the next part of our book tells you lots of things that can help you with the problems you checked off.

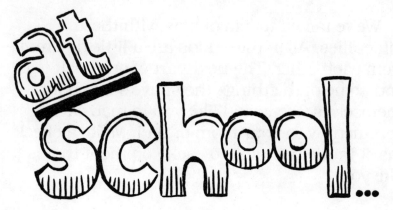

Teachers are always telling me,
"Slow down. Don't rush!"

When I'm at school it's hard to keep
sitting at my desk.

I have trouble finishing my assignments.

I have trouble remembering to bring
home permission slips and homework
assignments.

When the teacher gives directions I
forget what she said.

Even when I try to listen, sometimes I
start daydreaming.

Sometimes I get in trouble for talking!

with my friends...

Sometimes I get mad at my friends.

I don't know why, but sometimes other kids don't want to play with me.

Most of my friends are younger than I am.

My mom or dad tells me I'm too bossy with other kids.

Some kids in my class pick on me and tease me.

I wish I had more friends.

I sometimes butt into other kids' games.

about myself...

Sometimes I think I'm not
as smart as other kids.

I wish I didn't get so hyper.

Sometimes I think something is
wrong with me, but I don't know what.

I get confused a lot.

Sometimes I feel different
from other kids.

No matter how hard I try,
somebody still gets mad at me.

I don't know why kids
tease me so much.

Sometimes when I'm playing I don't hear my parents call me.

My room is usually in a big mess.

I like to do exciting stuff. My parents are always telling me to be more careful.

Lots of times I forget when my mom or dad tells me to do something.

I *hate* to do homework.

When I'm at home I usually finish my dinner before everybody else, and I want to get up from the table.

I make mistakes and then people get
mad at me.

Now you've checked off all the things that you think apply to you. Some kids check off almost all of the items. Other kids check only some of them.

Some kids who have trouble paying attention are very active and can't sit still for long. Like this:

Other kids are pretty quiet and inactive and daydream a lot. Like this:

Do you think you are more like the active kids or more like the daydreamers? What does your mom or dad think? Whether you're active or quiet, you could have trouble paying attention, being organized, and remembering things.

It may feel like you've checked off a lot of problems in this section, but ...

Many other kids have these problems too. The rest of our book tells about how other people can help you and how you can help yourself.

If you're like a lot of kids who helped us write
this book you're getting a little tired of reading
right now. That's OK. (Whenever you're reading
or doing schoolwork you will get more done if you
give yourself a break after about 15 minutes.)
Why don't you take a break now and see if you
can help our superhero find his homework. We
bet you know how he feels!

PART TWO

THINGS THAT OTHER PEOPLE CAN DO TO HELP ME

feel better after your break?

That's a good habit to learn. Work for a while, then take a short break.

Now that you have read this far in our book, you and your mom or dad probably have a pretty good idea whether or not you are like some of the kids in this book.

To really know whether you need special help, you should have an evaluation. The evaluation is kind of fun. You and your parents will answer questions like the ones in this book. You might put puzzles together, play memory games, and all sorts of other stuff. If you have already been evaluated, then this book is *definitely for you!*

Now, let's look at ways your parents and other people can help you learn to pay better attention.

Someone who really understands your problems might go to your school and talk to your teacher about ways to help you to become a better student.

For some kids, it has helped to go to a classroom which is quieter and which has fewer kids. In a smaller class kids can concentrate better and can also get more help from the teacher.

Sometimes it is helpful for kids to be in a group that teaches them to make friends and to get along better with other kids.

Another thing which can help is to meet with a counselor once in a while (or even every week!) and talk about things that have been happening in your life.

You can tell your counselor about problems you have at home or at school and the counselor never fusses at you and never says it's all your fault.

In fact, the counselor will help you figure out what to do about it the next time something bad starts to happen.

Counseling can help you understand yourself better and feel more confident about yourself, too. If you go to counseling, it would be a good idea to take this book with you to your counselor. You could show your counselor the things you checked off in the first part of this book, and your counselor could help you figure out what to do.

Sometimes, you might talk to the counselor along with your parents and your brothers or sisters. This usually happens when there are some problems that need to be solved by the whole family.

Another thing that can help is for your parents to talk with a special teacher or counselor. The counselor can teach your parents better ways to help you get ready for school in the morning, easier ways to get you though your homework, and better ideas for helping you when you feel angry or frustrated.

Your parents will also learn that you haven't been just lazy or bad. They'll learn that you really have been trying, but that it's hard for you to do what everybody wants you to do.

Some kids go to a doctor who gives them special medicine which helps them calm down and pay better attention. Usually the medicine is called Ritalin, but sometimes it has other names. Taking medicine doesn't mean you are sick. The medicine just gives your body what it needs to help you pay better attention.

Many kids who take medicine are able to get their schoolwork done more easily. It can also help kids get along better with other kids.

Not all kids who have difficulty paying attention take medicine, though. Your parents, your counselor, and your doctor will decide if they think it might help you.

So you can see there are lots of different ways that people can help you. You are probably ready for another break. How would you like to help our mouse connect the dots?

PART THREE

THINGS I CAN DO
TO HELP MYSELF

OK. You have just learned about many ways that *other* people can help you. But you can also do lots of things to help yourself. On the next pages are some ideas that *you* can try at home or at school. You'll need to talk about them with your parents and your teacher so that they can help you.

Lots of kids have trouble remembering things. Sometimes it helps to repeat what you've learned out loud. We've just talked about 6 ways other people can help you. How many can you remember?

1. _____

2. _____

3. _____

4. _____

5. _____

6. _____

You probably won't remember them all the first time. If you can't, just go back and check. This is a good way to remember important things. Try this approach with your schoolwork, too!

1. Read it.
2. Try to remember it.
3. Go back and check.

1. Someone could talk to your teacher.
2. A smaller, quieter classroom could help.
3. You could be in a group with other kids.
4. You could meet with a counselor.
5. Your parents could meet with a counselor.
6. The doctor could prescribe medicine.

Homework

"Yuck! I hate homework!" If this sounds like you, here are some helpful hints for kids who have trouble getting their homework done:

Find a place to do homework that isn't near a lot of temptations like TVs or stereos.

If you need help with your homework, sometimes the kitchen table is a good place to work.

Pick a study time and stick to it. Homework is easier if it's a regular habit.

Sometimes it is easier to memorize something if you move around. Try marching around the table while you memorize math facts or spelling words.

Don't try to do too much at one time. Work for 15 minutes, take a short break, then work some more.

getting ready in the morning!

The best way to get ready in the morning is to do as much as you can the night before. That way, if something is lost, you'll have time to look for it.

Put out your clothes the night before. Pack your lunch the night before, and get together everything you'll need to take to school the next day.

In the morning, get a regular routine going. Doing things in the same order each morning makes it easier to get it done.

Make a check list of what to do each morning and put it on the wall where you will see it.

Don't play or watch TV until you're completely ready!

Get your mom or dad to set up a "launching pad." This is a place for you to put everything you'll take to school the next day. Make a list to put up near your launching pad so that you can remind yourself of what you need.

I forgot!

If forgetting things and losing things is one of your problems, here are some helpful hints for improving your memory:

Don't kid yourself and say you'll do it later. Make "Do it now" the rule you live by.

Get in the habit of writing notes to yourself. Yellow stickpads are great because you can stick notes where you will be sure to see them. Maybe your mom or dad can get you some.

Always put things away in the same place.

Learn to *stop and think* for a minute before you rush out the door. *"Let's see, have I got everything I need?"*

Review your day when you wake up. "Let's see, today is Tuesday, so I have soccer practice after school."

Ways to pay better attention at school ...

Sit close to the front of the class and look at your teacher whenever he or she is talking.

Get involved! Don't just sit there. Ask questions, make comments (after raising your hand, of course).

Ask to be moved away from kids who talk or bother you.

When you catch your mind wandering, bring it back to class!

When you miss a little of what your teacher says, raise your hand and ask. Don't just sit there feeling confused. If you do, your mind will wander even more.

Don't bring things to school or play with things at your desk that will distract you.

learning to control yourself

When you're really frustrated and feel like you might "lose it," try the *calm down exercise*. It has three parts.

1. Think of something you like, like going to the beach or riding your bike. Try to get a good picture of this in your mind.

2. Take a deep breath and let it out *very slowly*.

3. Think the words "calm down."

OK, go ahead and try it. First think of something nice... Now, take a deep breath and let it out **slowly**... and think "calm down." Now, do it two more times.

You did it. *Terrific!*

Remember, when you're really angry you need to take 3 deep breaths. Then, if you're still angry or frustrated, go find a parent or teacher to help you with your problem.

It helps to practice the "calm down exercise" in advance. Maybe your mother or father would practice it with you. It might help them, too!

Getting really frustrated and angry is a problem for lots of kids. In addition to the "calm down exercise," here are some other things you can do to keep from getting so angry or upset.

Get away from the person you're mad at so things don't get worse.

Go to a quiet place, if you can, to do the "calm down exercise."

If someone is trying to make you angry, tell yourself you're too smart the let *them* get *you* in trouble! Go tell your parent or your teacher about the problem.

Decide in advance to *stay away* from anyone who picks on you or tries to get you upset.

If something you're <u>doing</u>, like homework, is frustrating you, go ask for help right away, before you're really "fed up."

learning to ask for help...

What do you do when you're confused or when something is too hard for you? Some kids feel embarrassed if they don't know what to do, so they just sit there and don't let anyone know. This just makes the problem worse. It's OK if you catch yourself not listening or not understanding. Just go to your teacher or your mother or father and say something like:

"I forgot what you asked me to do."

or

"I still don't understand what to do."

or

"Will you help me with this?"

Explain to your teacher that you are trying hard. Tell your teacher that one way you help yourself is to make sure you understand what you need to do.

Problem Solving

What do you do when you have a problem? For really big problems you may need the help of a parent or teacher, but sometimes you can figure out what to do all by yourself if you use these steps. It's called "problem solving."

Step 1: What's the problem?

Step 2: What are some of the things I could do about it?

Step 3: Which thing seems the best to do?

Step 4: Try out your idea and see if it works.

Step 5: If it doesn't work, try another idea.

Think of a problem you have now, or that you've had in the past few days. Try "problem solving" using all five steps and see if you can think of a solution you haven't found before. Maybe your mom or dad could help you practice "problem solving."

Boy, that's a lot of stuff to try and learn how to do!

Yes, it is. We've talked about ways to get your homework done, getting ready in the morning, improving your memory, paying better attention at school, learning to control yourself, learning to ask for help, and becoming a problem-solver!

Don't expect to learn how to do all of these things at once. You and your parents should pick one project and work on it a while. When it gets easier, then start a new project.

We've talked about many things you may want to change, but it's important for you and your parents to remember there are lots of things about you that are already *terrific.*

On the next page, why don't you and your parents make up a list of some of the great things about you.

_____

_____

_____

_____

_____

_____

_____

_____

_____

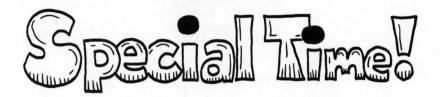

Special Time!

Another way for you to feel good about youself is to have a *special time* for a few minutes each day with your mom or dad.

A *special time* is a time just for fun. It should be a few minutes when nobody corrects you, criticizes you, or reminds you of *anything*. It should be a time when you don't worry about trying to learn something that's hard for you. Your mom or dad might have a hard time at first remembering not to correct you or remind you of anything. (See, you're not the only one who needs to learn new ways to behave!)

Maybe you could talk with your mom or dad about having a *special time* together starting today. You could talk, go for a walk, play a game, or do an activity together. The important thing is

for you and your parent to relax and just enjoy being together.

We've covered many things in this book. We hope that you've learned a lot and had some fun, too.

If you and your parents try some of the ideas we've talked about, we think it can help you. These ideas have helped *lots* of other kids and we are happy we can share them with you.

So, keep up the good work and...

WORD FINDER GAME

```
A D I S T R A C T I B L E C
T R X L L I K S R Y M J P A
T O C T I V E F Y S S E M L
E U W U Z O R G A N I Z E M
N T B W K Q J F R I E N D O
T I U C R K X I P S J T Q C
I N S J O V T E A C H E R E
O E Y X W N J Y S H Z G P V
N D O N E F V P V O F R L I
H H R T M W L Z H O C O A T
D D T Z O E E K I L Q F Y C
A A F Q H V O L I S T E N A
```

SCHOOL	ADHD	HOMEWORK
ATTENTION	TEACHER	ORGANIZE
DISTRACTIBLE	ACTIVE	ROUTINE
TRY	HELPS	CALM
LISTEN	FORGET	DONE
LIKE	BUSY	MESSY
PLAY	FRIEND	SKILL

PART FOUR

SPECIAL PROJECT FUN

An Important Note to Parents:

Changing habits is <u>hard</u> work. Kids need incentives (not bribes) just as adults do. To help your child succeed, you may want to agree on a reward for getting positive checks ("getting better" and "super job"). These don't have to be expensive nor should they be rewards you don't want to give your child. They need to be rewards you both feel good about. Here are some suggestions other parents have used:

Board game with parent

Bake cookies

Friend over after school

Friend for overnight on weekend

Dinner at McDonalds

Pizza delivery

Computer game with parent

Play ball with parent for 20 minutes

Not having to do a particular chore one night

Staying up an extra 15-30 minutes one night

Get a simple science experiment book and
    let child select one to do with parent

A movie rental and popcorn

Help mom make a special, much-desired snack

Phone gets plugged into jack in child's room
    for a couple of hours

Always be generous with social reinforcers:

smiles	"well done"
hugs	"thanks"
pats on the back	"good try"
"I like that"	"you're terrific"

These are the real self-esteem builders, even
when it does not appear that your child notices.

An Important Note to Kids:

We've talked about working on a lot of new habits, but you can't work on them all at once. We suggest that you sit down with your parents or counselor and choose the project you want to work on first. Then write the name of that project at the top of the page that says Week #1 - I'm working on _____. Each night sit down with your mom or dad and discuss how well you did that day on your project. Make a check mark in the spot you think describes your success that day.

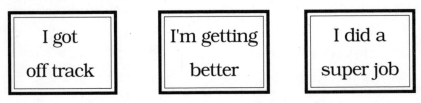

| I got off track | I'm getting better | I did a super job |

<u>Don't</u> expect all "super jobs" - nobody is perfect and nobody changes all at once.

If you keep getting "off-track" try some "problem-solving" to figure out what the problem is and what to do about it. Maybe your mom or dad can help you figure out how to do better.

(Parents – Feel free to copy these project sheets for your child to work on developing new habits.)

WEEK # ___   I'M WORKING ON ___

HOW AM I DOING?

	OFF TRACK	GETTING BETTER	SUPER JOB
DAY 1	☐	☐	☐
DAY 2	☐	☐	☐
DAY 3	☐	☐	☐
DAY 4	☐	☐	☐
DAY 5	☐	☐	☐
DAY 6	☐	☐	☐
DAY 7	☐	☐	☐

PROBLEM SOLVING: When I'm trying to ___
but I get off track...

What's the problem? ___

What are some things I can try to solve
the problem?

1.
2.
3.

WEEK # ____   I'M WORKING ON _____

HOW AM I DOING?

	OFF TRACK	GETTING BETTER	SUPER JOB
DAY 1	☐	☐	☐
DAY 2	☐	☐	☐
DAY 3	☐	☐	☐
DAY 4	☐	☐	☐
DAY 5	☐	☐	☐
DAY 6	☐	☐	☐
DAY 7	☐	☐	☐

PROBLEM SOLVING: When I'm trying to _____
but I get off track...
   What's the problem? _____

What are some things I can try to solve
the problem?
   1.
   2.
   3.

WEEK # ____   I'M WORKING ON ____

HOW AM I DOING?

	OFF TRACK	GETTING BETTER	SUPER JOB
DAY 1	☐	☐	☐
DAY 2	☐	☐	☐
DAY 3	☐	☐	☐
DAY 4	☐	☐	☐
DAY 5	☐	☐	☐
DAY 6	☐	☐	☐
DAY 7	☐	☐	☐

PROBLEM SOLVING: When I'm trying to ____
but I get off track ...

What's the problem? ____

What are some things I can try to solve
the problem?

1.
2.
3.

Parents:

There are several organizations which parents of children with attention deficits can join. One of these is Ch.A.D.D. (Children with Attention Deficit Disorder). Although only a few years old, it has grown so rapidly that it has local chapters all over the nation. Ch.A.D.D. hosts a large, comprehensive annual convention, bringing together parents, professionals, and leaders in the field of attention deficit disorders.

To join Ch.A.D.D., write to:

Ch.A.D.D.
499 Northwest 70th Avenue
Suite 308
Plantation, Florida 33317
(305) 587-3700

The National Ch.A.D.D. office can inform you of the location of your nearest Ch.A.D.D. chapter. These groups usually meet once a month to provide information and support.

Another national organization is ADDA (Attention Deficit Disorder Association). To join, write:

Membership Chair
ADDA
2620 Ivy Place
Toledo, Ohio 43613
(419) 472-1286

Both of these organizations have newsletters which will keep you informed regarding new books, new research, and new services.

We encourage you to join one or both of these. The better informed you are as a parent, the more you will be able to help your child.

Below is a list of books you may find helpful:

ADD, Attention Deficit Disorder, Glenn Hunsucker,
    Forresst Publishing, 1988.

Attention Deficit Hyperactivity Disorder,
    Russell A. Barkley, Guilford Publications, Inc., 1990.

Defiant Children, Russell A. Barkley, Ph. D.,
    Guilford Press, 1987.

Developmental Variation and Learning Disorders, Melvin D.
    Levine M.D., Educators Publishing Service, Inc., 1987.

High School Help for ADD Teens, Ellen B. Dixon, Ph.D. and
    Kathleen G. Nadeau, Ph.D., Chesapeake Psychological
    Publications, 5041 A&B Backlick Road, Annandale, VA.
    22003, 1993.

How to Talk So Kids Will Listen & Listen So Kids Will Talk,
    Adele Faber and Elaine Mazlish, Avon Books, 1980.

Hyperkinetic Children: A Neuropsychological Approach,
    C. Keith Conners, Sage Publications, Inc., 1986.

Keeping a Head in School, Levine, Mel D., M.D.,
    Educators Publishing Service, Inc., 1990.

My Brother's A World-Class Pain, Gardner, Michael, Ph.D.,
    GSI Publications, P.O. Box 746, DeWitt, N.Y., 13214.

Negotiating Parent/Adolescent Conflict,
    Arthur L. Robin, Guilford Press, 1989.

Otto Learns About His Medicine: A Story About Medication
    for Hyperactive Children, Matthew Galvin M.D.,
    Magination Press, 1988.

Putting on the Brakes, Quinn, Patricia O., M.D., and Stern,
    Judith, M.A., Brunner/Mazel - Magination Press, 1991.

Shelly the Hyperactive Turtle, Moss, Deborah,
    Woodbine House, 1989.

Stop and Think Workbook, Philip C. Kendall, Ph.D.,
    238 Meeting House Lane, Merion Station, PA 19066.

Taming The Tornado In Your Classroom And At Home,
    Dr. Allan Lifson, Educational Consultant Group,
    729 West 16th St., Suite B-3, Costa Mesa, CA. 92627.

The ADD Hyperactivity Handbook for Schools,
    Parker, Harvey C., Ph.D., Impact Publications, Florida, 1992.

The ADD Hyperactivity Workbook for Parents, Teachers, and Kids,
    Parker, Harvey C., Ph.D., Impact Publications, Florida, 1988.

The ADHD Child in the Classroom: Strategies for the Regular
    Classroom Teacher, Martin, Lucy C., M.Ed., and the staff of
    Chesapeake Psychological Publications, 5041 A&B Backlick
    Road, Annandale, VA. 22003, 1991.

Hyperactive Child, Adolescent and Adult, Paul H. Wender, M.D.,
    Oxford University Press, 1987.

The Misunderstood Child, Larry B. Silver, M.D., McGraw Hill, 1984.

Your Hyperactive Child: A Parent's Guide to Coping With Attention
    Deficit Disorder, Barbara Ingersoll, Ph.D., Doubleday, 1988.

About the Authors

Kathleen Nadeau has practiced psychology in the Washington, D.C. area since 1970. Her interest in attentional problems is personal, as well as professional. She hopes that this book and others like it will make the going easier for children growing up today. Kathleen lives with her family in Silver Spring, Maryland where her home is paved with Post-It™ note reminders.

Ellen B. Dixon has been a psychotherapist for over twenty years, specializing in the everyday adjustment problems of children and adults. Over the last few years she has become increasingly involved in the diagnosis and treatment of attention deficit-related problems. Ellen works in an office with two desks and a credenza, which helps to keep her own attention and organizational problems under control.

About the Artist

John R. Rose is the Staff Artist/Cartoonist for <u>The Warren Sentinel</u> newspaper in Front Royal, Virginia. He created the children's cartoon/ activity page, "Kids' Home Newspaper," which is syndicated by Copley News Service. His <u>Sentinel</u> editorial cartoons, illustrations and news graphics have won over 30 awards from the Virginia Press Association. John's editorial cartoons are syndicated nationally by Associated Features.